DEFEAT THE SPECTE OF DEPRESSION

A short book on how to overcome Depression.

By. HAJAR EL FETTAHI

Content

***H**ello, I'm depression, I'm a good disease, you can't leave me now, I embody your soul and take it far, so you have to think and stay away from joy, so the more I feel about death, the more I rejoice, because I want to kill you slowly, I just want your soul to come out and go to the sky far away. But what kills me the most is will and determination and passion.*

Chapter one:

What is Depression?

"Depression is when brilliant people fall into a trap"

Depression is not just a temporary sadness over the death of someone dear, or that drop in mood that we feel from time to time, and not just a feeling of loneliness while visiting someone close or exchanging a conversation with a friend.

When depression is mentioned, mention with it many characteristics of mental disorder, including mood Turbidity, pessimism, helplessness, slow thought processes, and the selection of sad and humiliating memories.

What we used to have joy in the recent past, today no longer carries anything but feelings of sorrow and sadness.

Depression is a mixture of sadness, loneliness, rejection feeling rejected by others, feeling helpless, and unable to cope with life's problems.

As defined by the American Institute of mental health, Depression is:

An imbalance in the rest of the body, including the body, thoughts, and mood, and affects the person's view of himself and the people around him and the events that happen, so that the patient loses his physical, psychological and emotional balance. Also, depression makes a person lose the ability to enjoy life, a feeling of frustration and hopelessness, in addition to trying to reach happiness and failure in that.

For me dear reader, I find Depression is a disorder that arises from overthinking about negative things that sneak into your mind, then you enter a state of intense sadness.

You will think that it is another bad day, but it is not. You will try to wear a mask that reflects your depressed personality.

It will be a mask full of joy and laughter, and you will try to be social, but you are actually drained and tiring, sad.

You will change a lot, you will no longer be a loving and cheerful person, you will hate the things you used to love, you will never care about anything anymore, you will prefer loneliness and isolation from the people around you, you will hate meeting someone, you will sleep.

a lot just because you do not want to live this painful reality, it is a deadly disease that creeps in for your life little by little and then its scales will turn, you will cry alone and do not want anyone to see you.

Depression is like internal bleeding that no one sees, but it exhausts its owner to the point of death. You will hate yourself and then your life and will try to commit suicide. You will wish to die over and over before bed. You will cry, but everyone will think that you are asleep.

You want to scream without anyone hearing you, you cry without anyone seeing you. You try to explain to anyone, but they will not understand. Do you know why?

Because they did not go through what you are going through, all these circumstances are important lectures from life to learn how to become stronger, even if you are convinced that you are weak, you will fight and fight and lose and repeat the loss once,

twice, three, until you succeed.
…...

chapter two

Symptoms of depression.

"Depression starts small and gets bigger little by little until it takes over your life, so be careful."

Many people get depressed without even knowing it. They believe that the symptoms they are suffering are part of normal mood swings.

Depression may be classified as mild, moderate, or severe based on the severity of symptoms, including:

Despair: from the future and all things, suffering from a severe loss of hope, and not looking at things positively at all.

Excessive emotions: such as rapid anger, extreme sadness, or passively standing about things that do not deserve attention.

Not being able to enjoy: even the things that previously appealed to the person and caused him to be happy and satisfied. The depressed no longer care about any of these former pleasures.

intense grief: which does not stop and does not have a specific cause. Rather, the depressed translates it many times with unjustified crying.

Fatigue: the depressed suffers from a lack of physical activity and an unwillingness to make any effort, but rather tends to sleep a lot.

Self-abasement: blaming it for all things, even those that are not the person's fault.

Dispersion of focus: the depressed suffers from a dispersion of focus, attention, and memorization.

Eating and sleeping disorders: One of the signs that a person has depression, such as losing his appetite for food completely or becoming an excessive appetite that cannot be controlled.

Dispersion of focus: the depressed suffers from a distraction in focus, attention, and memorization.

Change in appetite and body weight: A person with depression may lose his appetite and lose weight, or his appetite and weight may increase.

Irresponsible behaviours: such as drinking excessively or indulging in gambling and irresponsible relationships sound.

lose self-confidence: Loss of self-esteem where thoughts such as inferiority and insignificance are common, and the person no longer trusts his ability to survive.

self-criticism: Self-criticism without reasonable cause or feeling unfounded guilt.

__Feelings of extreme guilt:__ Guilt often appears related to situations that are not One can control it or in situations that are not He hadn't done anything wrong.

__dark thoughts:__ The depressed person's mind harbours thoughts of death and even wishes, and they also have suicidal thoughts.

__Feelings of hesitation and inability to focus:__ The person is no longer able to focus or act towards Some things that he always felt were automatic

__Agitation:__ The depressed person becomes either paralyzed or disturbingly hyperactive

__sleep disruption:__ The sleep disorder in a depressed person is difficulty falling asleep or interrupted sleep and waking up during the early hours of the day, or it may be oversleeping.

In addition, symptoms of depression may differ completely from one person to another. Sometimes depression is vague physical pain and discomfort, which is difficult to detect. Moreover, a person with depression may be unable to describe his feelings to people close to him or to health care professionals. He may talk about personal relationships, sleep problems, financial or health problems rather than depression.

…..

chapter three:

Types of depression.

"Depression is not a weakness; it is a sign of your strength for a long time."

It is important to know the different types of depression, as this knowledge helps to build a complete perception of the diagnosis of the disease. Thus, I will present to you, dear reader, the most prominent types of depression:

Smiling depression: It is that a person suffers from depression and bad mood, and is keen to appear

He is happy in front of others and loses his sense of happiness in anything he does, and one of the symptoms of this disease is excessive eating, as well as sleeping for long hours, and the feeling of this type of depression grows in the evening period.

Teen depression: Persons grow physically, psychologically, and socially rapidly during adolescence, and this stage is one of the important stages in the development of mental health and some symptoms may appear as depression in early childhood,

and people at this stage have a feeling of insomnia, self-obliteration, and behavioural disorders, however, the likelihood of seizures increases Depression is highly significant during and shortly after puberty, and people during this period adopt intense feelings and feel depressed and sad sometimes, but depression differs from these mood changes associated with adulthood disorders.

Symptoms of depression vary between adults and young people, one of the most obvious symptoms among young people is:

irritability and anger, not actual depression, and according to the above, adolescents experience the same feelings of depressed adults such as losing interest in things that previously interested them, and depression may become in adolescents, especially when it changes Their behaviours is significantly greater compared to their previous behaviours. Girls are more likely to be depressed than boys, or at least girls are more likely to be diagnosed with depression, knowing that social support is a very important factor for a depressed teenager.

In addition, good relationships with friends and parents help in the recovery process, and many young people who Sufferers from depression also complain of another problem at the same time. These problems are likely to be drug abuse, attention deficit, and behavioural disorders, as well as eating disorders and anxiety. It is worth noting that there is an effective range of treatment methods available for all these problems.

In addition, good relationships with parents and friends contribute to recovery from this type of depression.

Seasonal Affective Disorder (SAD): Seasonal affective disorder (SAD) describes a period of depression or low mood associated with a particular time of the year with changing seasons. Symptoms often begin in November and disappear in the spring. It is called seasonal depression.

However, Seasonal affective disorder can occur in the summer or spring, although this is less common. Affective disorder is more prevalent among women, and the age of onset ranges between twenty and thirty years, but symptoms may appear earlier than this.

SAD can affect even people who don't have depression or mood disorders, and symptoms vary from severe to mild for different people.

Seasonal affective disorder likely results from less exposure to sunlight during the winter months, because there are fewer daylight hours, and on cloudy winter days there is almost no sun. The distance from the equator (that is, the colder the weather) increases the risk of infection.

Having a family history of depression or suicide can be an additional risk factor for a mood disorder.

Because seasonal affective disorder has an expected pattern of recurrence, preventive measures may help reduce symptoms. Some forms of prevention that can help are increasing the amount of light in the home, meditation and other stress management techniques, spending more time outside, and visiting sunny places.

post-partum depression: Many mothers become somewhat more emotional after the birth process, at least, and the emotionality is often characterized by crying, mood swings, distress, sleep problems, and appetite, where the child feels strange and the mother may not feel what she wants, and often the mother's love for her baby increases little by little. Unrealistic expectations and childhood stories that represent the most beautiful moments in a mother's life create strong feelings of guilt.

Postpartum agitation is normal, as it arises as a result of changes caused by the birth of the child and the experience of childbirth as well as hormonal changes, and most importantly also that a mother who appears after birth needs understanding and support from those close to her and health care workers.

Diagnosing postpartum depression is a good thing. Actual postpartum depression requires treatment, and there is a fine line between irritability and depression, and sometimes depression develops slowly, knowing that postpartum depression develops within one year of the birth process, and its symptoms are similar to episodes of depression. For another, and with the mother's fatigue, lack of experience, and anxiety, she may have obsessive thoughts, fears, and concerns related to the child and his care, such as the mother thinking, for example, about harming her infant.

Although these fears are rarely justified, it is always important to seek help to recover from postpartum depression, and this type of depression often involves feelings of guilt without any basis, and this prevents the mother from seeking help at first, as it may She thinks that she cannot reveal her feelings of depression to others, because everyone thinks that she is happy with her baby, yet this depression represents a mental disorder that has nothing to do with how much the mother loves her baby, so we can say that a diagnosis of postpartum depression is a good thing.

Aging -depression: Changes in health and life situations caused by old age can put pressure on mental health.

Depression often occurs in older people as a result of losing a friend or family member, as well as deteriorating personal physical health, along

with loneliness, which represents a heavy burden on the mental health of many of them.

Symptoms of depression are not easily noticed in the elderly. On the one hand, many symptoms of depression, such as sleep disturbances, fatigue, and anorexia, are considered natural changes that accompany age, and on the other hand, the condition of elderly people with dementia improves significantly once depression is discovered and treated, knowing that isolation Vague pains, delusions and memory disturbances may become signs of depression and other illnesses.

depression may be difficult to detect in older people. if they are trying to improve because of negative personal images and fears associated with mental disorders.

Bipolar Disorder (Manic Depression):

bipolar disorder is when you experience periods where you alternate between exhilaration and depression, with normal periods in between. These moods are called hypomania, mania, and depression. There are various combinations of moods that are divided into different types of bipolar disorder. Bipolar disorder may be triggered by external events, stress, and general sources of strain. It begins to appear in adolescence. It is a lifelong illness.

The risk of developing bipolar disorder is one to two percent, and it is equally common around the world.

Mania and hypomania can impair your judgment, which affects relationships, work, and your financial situation. For example, you may begin multiple projects, experience euphoria and become excessively extroverted and do things with more or less serious consequences.

You are often extremely active and need very little sleep. Your self-confidence is considerably greater than usual, and you may become irritated if someone questions your brilliant ideas, romantic infatuations, nightlife, and all of the projects you have started, for example: During a manic episode, you are more intense, it is easy for you to lose touch with reality and you may develop psychoses. During a hypomanic episode, you do not lose touch with reality and you are less intense. You suffer depression after episodes of mania and hypomania. The depression may be so severe that you experience suicidal thoughts and make plans to commit suicide.

Sometimes these thoughts are so difficult that you attempt suicide.

Both a manic and a hypomanic episode include these symptoms:

-Increased activity, energy, or agitation

-Exaggerated sense of well-being and self-confidence (euphoria)

-Unusual talkativeness

-Racing thoughts

-Distractibility

-being easily distracted

-having overconfidence in your abilities

-Poor decision-making

The exact cause of bipolar disorder is unknown, but some factors may include:

Biological differences: People with bipolar disorder appear to have organic changes in the brain. The significance of these changes remains uncertain but may eventually help identify the causes.

Genetic factors: bipolar disorder is more common in people who have first-degree relatives with the disease, such as siblings or parents.

 Researchers are also trying to find genes that may cause bipolar disorder.

Psychotic depression: Psychotic depression includes symptoms of clinical depression, such as sadness, hopelessness, apathy, and lack of initiative. Besides, psychotic symptoms appear with psychotic episodes at a variable level.

Psychotic symptoms that appear as part of psychotic depression are of two types.

The first type includes psychotic symptoms that match depressive characteristics. For example, muteness (aphasia), severe self-neglect, and delusions that correspond to feelings of sadness and despair. For example, thoughts about a voice telling the person that it is worthless. The second type includes psychotic symptoms that contrast with depressive symptoms. Thus, for example, a person may feel depressed, and at the same time have a sense of grandiosity, the feeling that he has extensive knowledge and excessive power.

Persistent Depressive Disorder: Persistent depressive disorder is a severe, disabling disorder. Its symptoms are similar to other types of clinical depression. It generally occurs less severe and more chronic than major depression. Persistent depressive disorder was referred to in earlier versions of the Diagnostic and Statistical Manual as partial depression, mild depression, or dysthymia.

Persistent depressive disorder is characterized by

being in a depressed mood all the time for at least two years. It may cause irritability in children and adults rather than gloomy moods.

This depression or nervous mood must be accompanied by any of the following: insomnia, excessive sleep, fatigue, decreased activity, low self-esteem, loss of appetite, binge eating, decreased concentration, or hesitation, or feeling hopeless.

Symptoms of major depression include anhedonia. It also includes psychomotor symptoms such as: Lethargy, drowsiness, or constant agitation, thoughts of death or suicide, anger, stress, feelings of guilt, sleeping for long hours, and changes in eating patterns.

These symptoms are often lower in persistent depressive disorder

Premenstrual Depression (PMS): Some women get depressed sometimes during the month for no apparent reason, then the time for the menstrual cycle comes in a few days, and this depression disappears. We may all have had this experience, even if we are quiet personalities, but sometimes

we become angry and depressed because of this bad psychological state, which is known as premenstrual depression.

Symptoms of PMS occur a week before the menstrual cycle most of the time, during which the woman feels sad, feeling unjustified anger, excessive nervousness, mood changes, a desire to

cry and lack of focus, exhaustion, and fatigue, which affects her work and personal life, then these symptoms disappear once the period begins the woman's mood returns to normal.

Premenstrual depression occurs due to hormonal changes that the body goes through, as serotonin decreases, which is known as the hormone of happiness.

....

Chapter four:

Causes of depression.

" You feel like you are a loser" It's just a feeling and not a fact, the truth is that you are frustrated with your reality frustrated with your attempts..."

The exact cause of depression is not known, However, research points to several factors that appear to increase the risk of developing or worsening depression, including:

chronic illness: In some people, a chronic illness causes depression. A chronic illness is an illness that lasts for a very long time and usually cannot be cured completely. However, chronic illnesses can often be controlled through diet, exercise, lifestyle habits, and certain medications. Some examples of chronic illnesses that may cause depression are diabetes, heart disease, arthritis,

kidney disease, HIV/AIDS, lupus, and multiple sclerosis (MS).

Hypothyroidism may also lead to depressed feelings.

Researchers believe that treating the depression may sometimes also help the co-existing medical illness improve.

Is Depression Linked to Chronic Pain?

When pain lingers for weeks to months, it's referred to as being "chronic." Not only does chronic pain hurt, it also disturbs your sleep, your ability to exercise

and be active in your relationships and your productivity at work.

You can see now how chronic pain may also leave you feeling sad, isolated, and depressed

Genes: Depression can sometimes run in families. This suggests that there's at least a partial genetic link to depression. Children, siblings, and parents of people with severe depression are somewhat more likely to suffer from depression than are members of the general population.

Multiple genes interacting with one another in special ways probably contribute to the various types of depression that run in families.

Yet despite the evidence of a family link to depression, it is unlikely that there is a single "depression" gene, but rather, many genes that each contribute small effects toward depression when they interact with the environment.

Drugs: Can Certain Drugs Cause Depression. In certain people, drugs may lead to depression. For example, medications such as barbiturates, benzodiazepines, and the acne drug isotretinoin (formerly sold as Accutane, now Absorica, Amnesteem, Claravis, Myorisan, Zenatane) have sometimes been associated with depression, especially in older people.

Likewise, medications such as corticosteroids, opioids (codeine, morphine), and anticholinergics are taken to relieve stomach cramping can sometimes cause changes and fluctuations in mood.

Birth control pills: Like any medication, the Pill can have side effects. Oral contraceptives contain a synthetic version of progesterone, which studies suggest can lead to depression in some women. The reason is still unknown, says Hilda Hutcherson, MD, clinical professor of obstetrics and genecology at Columbia University, in New York. "It doesn't happen to everyone, but if women have a history of depression or are prone to depression, they have an increased chance of experiencing depression symptoms while taking birth control pills," Dr. Hutcherson says. "Some women just can't take the Pill; that's when we start looking into alternative contraception, like a diaphragm, which doesn't contain hormones."

Lack of fish in the diet: Low intake of omega-3 fatty acids, found in salmon and vegetable oils, may be associated with a greater risk of depression. A 2004 Finnish study found an association between eating less fish and depression in women, but not in men. These fatty acids regulate neurotransmitters like serotonin, which could explain the link. Fish oil supplements may work too; at least one study found they helped depression in people with bipolar disorder.

Poor sibling relationships: Although unhappy relationships with anyone can cause depression, a

2007 study in the American Journal of Psychiatry found that men who didn't get along with their siblings before age 20 were more likely to be depressed later in life than those who did. Although it's not clear what's so significant about sibling relationships (the same wasn't true for relationships with parents), researchers suggest that they could help children develop the ability to relate with peers and socialize. Regardless of the reason, too much squabbling is associated with a greater risk of developing depression before age 50.

Where you live: You can endlessly debate whether city or country life is better. But research has found that people living in urban settings do have a 39% higher risk of mood disorders than those in rural regions. A 2011 study in the journal Nature offers an explanation for this trend:

activity in the part of the brain that regulates stress. And higher levels of stress could lead to psychotic disorders. Depression rates also vary by country and state. Some states have higher rates

of depression and affluent nations having higher rates than low-income nations. Even altitude may play a role, with suicide risk going up with altitude.

Poor sleep habits: It's no surprise that sleep deprivation can lead to irritability, but it could also increase the risk of depression. A 2007 study found that when healthy participants were deprived of sleep, they had greater brain activity after viewing upsetting images than their well-rested counterparts, which is similar to the reaction that depressed patients have noted one of the study authors.

"If you don't sleep, you don't have time to replenish brain cells, the brain stops functioning well, and one of the many factors that could lead to is depression," says Matthew Edlund, MD, director of the Center for Circadian Medicine, in Sarasota, Fla., and author of The Power of Rest.

Thyroid disease: When the thyroid, a butterfly-shaped gland in the neck, doesn't produce enough

thyroid hormone, it's known as hypothyroidism, and depression is one of its symptoms. This hormone is multifunctional, but one of its main tasks is to act as a neurotransmitter and regulate serotonin levels. If you experience new depression symptoms-particularly along with cold sensitivity, constipation, and fatigue-a thyroid test couldn't hurt. Hypothyroidism is treatable with medication.

Smoking: Smoking has long been linked with depression, though it's a chicken-or-egg scenario: People who are depression-prone may be more likely to take up the habit. However, nicotine is known to affect neurotransmitter activity in the brain, resulting in higher levels of dopamine and serotonin (which is also, the mechanism of action for antidepressant drugs).

This may explain the addictive nature of the drug and the mood swings that come with withdrawal, as well as why depression is associated with smoking cessation.

Avoiding cigarettes and staying smoke free-could help balance your brain chemicals.

End of a TV show or movie: When something important comes to an end, like a TV show, movie, or a big home renovation, it can trigger depression in some people. In 2009, some Avatar fans reported feeling depressed and even suicidal because the movie's fictional world wasn't real. There was a similar reaction to the final installments of the Harry Potter movies. "People experience distress when they're watching primarily for companionship," said Emily Moyer-Guse, Ph.D., assistant professor of communication at Ohio State University, in Columbus. With Avatar, Moyer-Guse suspects people were "swept up in a narrative forgetting about real life and (their) own problems."

social media addiction: Spending too much time on social media. A number of studies now suggest that this can be associated with depression, particularly in teens and preteens. Internet addicts may struggle with real-life human interaction and a lack of companionship, and they may have an unrealistic view of the world.

Some experts even call it "social media depression". In a study, researchers found that about 1.2% of people ages 16 to 51 spent an inordinate amount of time online, and that they had a higher rate of moderate to severe depression.

However, the researchers noted that it is not clear if Internet overuse leads to depression or if depressed people are more likely to use the Internet.

R-X medicine: Depression is a side effect of many medicines. For example, Accutane and its generic version (isotretinoin) are prescribed to clear up severe acne, but depression and suicidal thoughts are a potential risk for some people. Depression is a possible side effect of anxiety and insomnia drugs, including Valium and Xanax, Lopressor, prescribed to treat high blood pressure, cholesterol-lowering drugs including Lipitor, and Premarin for menopausal symptoms.

Read the potential side effects when you take a new medication, and always check with your doctor to see if you might be at risk.

…..

Chapter five:

depression side effects.

"When you leave the field open to depression by controlling your thoughts, it will devour your beautiful memories first, and then occupy the space in which you hid your dreams, those dreams that you sacrificed so much to reach."

Depression is a severe and stressful illness that can place a heavy burden on individuals and families.

Untreated depression may worsen and deteriorate to the point of disability. Depression can lead to severe emotional, behavioural, health, and even legal and economic problems that affect all different areas of life:

Depression affects the brain structure: It is not only your body and your psyche that is affected by depression, but the shape of your mind and the structure of your brain also have their share. Depression. Another study, presented by the University of Michigan Depression Center, indicated that the receptors responsible for "the hormone serotonin, which in turn is responsible for happiness in the brain, are less in a depressed person than in a healthy person, The fewer these receptors, the greater the severity of depression.

Depression affects physical health: A recent study revealed that people who recover from strokes or heart attacks and become depressed have higher chances of the disease returning to them again, and they find it difficult to follow doctor's instructions, and another study found that patients who suffer from depression have higher chances of dying after a heart attack.

Depression affects depressed sleep:

Although the most common problem for a depressed person is insomnia or difficulty getting enough sleep, some depressed people feel an excessive need to sleep with a loss of energy, and depression may lead to weight gain or loss, feelings of hopelessness, helplessness, sensitivity, and depression treatment helps the person in controlling all of these symptoms.

Common signs of insomnia with depression include:

-Daytime fatigue.

_Sensitivity and difficulty concentrating.

_Not getting enough sleep, no matter how many hours you sleep.

_Trouble getting back to sleep after waking up at night.

_Waking up before the alarm goes off.

_Anxiety and waking up at night.

Depression leads to addiction: Drug and alcohol abuse is the most common thing for people suffering from depression, especially among teens and young adults, and these people should be helped because they are more likely to commit suicide.

Signs of drug or alcohol abuse include:

-Tremors

-Amnesia

_ Grief counselling

_Not wanting to talk about drugs or alcohol.

Depression affects your family: Since life with a depressed person is difficult and stressful for family members and friends, it is helpful to have a family member involved in the assessment and treatment of the depressed person.

Pregnancy depression affects the fetus: The mother's psychological state affects the child, not only after birth but while he is still a fetus. As the fetus grows, it constantly receives messages from its mother, hears her heartbeat, and receives chemical signals from the placenta. A new study from the Association for Psychological Sciences finds that signals about a mother's mental state affect her baby's development after birth. In a study conducted by two researchers at the University of California on the impact of the psychological state of the mother on the fetus, it was found that children with better and consistent performance were to mothers who were in good mental and physical health before and after birth, and children born to mothers suffering from depression before birth were slower in growth.

......

chapter six:

How to defeat depression?

"It ends when Strong will begins"

Do not think that medication is the solution to the state of depression that you are going through and that it will save you from that dark well in which you fell. Taking a daily tablet did not completely eliminate your despair. The solution that you must undergo is to follow the depression treatment plan, which is also applied in the treatment of addiction, which depends on changing yourself, your way of thinking, your lifestyle, and knowing the origins of depression and its treatment. You will succeed in a way you did not expect in saving you from that darkness and returning to your life again.

In fact, "medicine in psychiatry is not everything" is a sentence you should believe in now more than ever. It is just a step in the journey that treats the symptom and does not eradicate the disease from its roots, so the treatment plan that I will mention will spare you from any medications. Let me take you with me to find out:

know the causes of depression: Why are you depressed? A question that the psychiatrist will ask you when you visit him in order to find out the cause of depression because knowing the cause is almost half the solution. Knowing the reason will help you diagnose your condition and deal with it with another look.

Emptying the soul of sediment: This step is absolutely one of the most important steps, and it is highly recommended by psychotherapists, which is to talk about everything that concerns you and makes you anxious and depressed. There is a large percentage of those who think that they are mentally ill. In fact, they only need to talk and empty themselves of all those sediments that have accumulated day after day, until they become a burden that weighs them down and makes them very tired.

Some may not imagine the effectiveness of this technique and its feasibility in treating depression without medication, it actually contributes very significantly to getting rid of depression without side effects, but sometimes it serves as an integrated treatment program, at the end of which

you will be rid of depression once and for all. But for this mechanism or step, there are some tips from psychotherapists, and they must be taken to make this step a success, and they are as follows:

Do not try to talk with someone you consider to be the cause of your depression in some way. If you think that what you are in is because of a partner, lover or friend, do not try to apply this step with him, because its results will be completely opposite, and may even compound the bad Your mental state is greatly affected. You need to empty all the sediments and not leave any detail unless you take it out of your depths. I don't need someone to get excited about what you're going to say, and to initiate a defensive reaction about his positions.

You should turn to a completely neutral person, who is also ready to listen to you to the end without reacting to what you will say, whether it is negative or positive. Someone who listens to you until you empty all the deposits inside you that have accumulated due to the days and problems you faced, whether at work or with a partner or lover. To allow him to give his opinion on what you say or what concerns you and makes you depressed. At the same time, he advises you with complete impartiality, so that depression can be completely treated without medication.

Receiving Cognitive Behavioural Therapy (CBT): This therapy helps you change how you think (cognitive) and how you act (behavioural). These changes can help you feel better. Unlike some other speech therapies, it focuses on immediate problems and difficulties. Instead of focusing on the causes and symptoms of your past distress, this type of therapy looks at ways to improve your current state of mind.

The way it works is to help you understand the problems that are controlling you by breaking them down into small parts. This makes it easier for you to see how these problems relate to each other and how they affect you. These parts are: thoughts, feelings, physical feelings, actions

There are helpful and unhelpful ways to interact with most situations and it depends on how you think about it. For example, you had a tough day, got bored, and then went shopping.

While you are walking on the road, someone you know passes by and clearly ignores you.

For thoughts: You better think that, for example, he has a problem and is very angry, which led to his ignoring you, instead of thinking that he ignored you because he doesn't love you.

For feeling: You will feel interested and worried about him instead of feeling depressed, sad, and rejected

For physical feeling: You will feel that it is normal and thus you will feel comfortable instead of feeling that it is a humiliating thing. thus, you will feel stomach cramps, feeling sick.

For act: you will call him and make sure that he is okay instead of Go home and avoid him.

The same case led to two different results depending on how you think about it. How you think affected how you felt and what you did.

When you think in a negative way, you will find yourself judging the topic without evidence, which led to:

A number of uncomfortable feelings.

Unhelpful behaviour.

If you go home feeling depressed, chances are you'll still think about what happened and feel bad, but if you call this person, there's a good chance you'll feel better. If you don't, you will not have the opportunity to correct any misunderstanding about what this person has done and you will likely feel even worse.

Thinking negatively makes you go into a vicious circle that can make you feel bad, and it may create new situations that make you feel worse as well. You may begin to think of unreal things about yourself. This happens because when we are in a stressful state, we are more likely to rush to judgment and interpret things in an unhelpful way.

This therapy helps you break this vicious circle of confused thinking, feelings, and accompanying behaviour. When you see the parts of this sequence clearly, you can change them and thus change how you feel about them. (CBT) aims to take you to a certain extent so that you perform the treatment yourself. This will deduce your own ways to deal with such problems.

It can be done individually or with a group of people. It can also be done with self-help books or a computer program.

Set small goals that you want to achieve: Feeling frustrated and failing and not being able to do something that is controlling you so that it hinders you from doing the simplest things, you must break this cycle, set small goals that you want to achieve without anyone's help, and step by step and you will integrate into the cycle of life again and return to you the feeling of yourself.

Stop comparing yourself to others: It is annoying to see yourself less than those around you, you find them achieving successive successes and living their lives happily while you are buried under the rubble of depression, that thinking may increase your suffering more so you must stop it.

Take a special look at yourself and focus on yourself and feel your weaknesses and do not enter into comparisons with others, we both have talents and latent forces that help us succeed.

Identify the things that give the most value to your presence in your life: As depressed you look at life from a narrow hole, nothing satisfies you or makes you happy always everything is incomplete and bad and that increases your depression more, so decide to give value to yourself and what you have, dedicate a minute daily to look at the good things that happen to you and what you have, whether phone, car, wife and children, no health problems, work, to help your mind to think positive.

Change your diet: Follow a healthy diet, avoid processed foods and reduce caffeinated drinks. Caffeine may make it more difficult to fall asleep and stay asleep. With a lack of sleep, depression can worsen.

Include vitamin D in your diet and expose yourself daily to the sun. Pay attention to eating vegetables and fruits along with seafood, and nuts rich in omega-3 because they contribute to increasing the release of neurotransmitters responsible for happiness and thus alleviating the effects of depression.

Exercise is the best treatment for depression without medication: There is no doubt that it is difficult to motivate yourself to exercise when you are depressed, however, as we mentioned earlier, you should help yourself out of depression. Physical activity is a great way to treat depression without medication.

When you exercise, the body produces endorphins, and this substance improves mood and reduces stress. As we mentioned, it is not easy to ask a depressed person to exercise, but try to go out for a walk, even if it is a quarter of an hour every day. Especially in the open plains or in the forests, try as much as possible to be close to nature during exercise. Do not imagine the positive result that will be reflected in your mood.

remember:

Exercising for you is not intended to lose weight, not at all, the purpose is just to go outside and make your heart beat a little faster, which requires your lungs to work better to inhale oxygen. When your lungs work faster to provide oxygen to fuel your body as a result of the effort, this will make the flow of oxygen much greater than usual.

Nature, oxygen, accelerate blood circulation, moves muscles, burns, and sweats. All these things will make your mood much better than if you stayed in your room with yourself and your windows closed, and oxygen at a minimum rate.

Also, yoga and meditation exercises make them your companion because they will make you feel a great ability to relax and calm, by following these steps:

Sit comfortably.

Choose a quiet, noise-free place.

Close my eyes

Breathe deeply and focus on your body while breathing.

Exercising, yoga, walking, or running in nature on a continuous basis in addition to the diet that I mentioned above, all of these things will definitely be enough to treat depression without medication.

You must get rid of your isolation: A recently published study showed that good friendship protects you from depression. Good friends also help reduce the risk of heart disease and boost the immune system.

Also, protect you from stress and depression.

Psychiatrists recommend mixing with people who have psychological problems and overcoming them. It may be helpful to meet with others who suffer from depression.

This can help remove feelings of isolation and at the same time show you how others have overcome their difficulties. Finding that you can help others may help you too.

Improve your sleep system:

What makes you most depressed is your inability to sleep well, the night turns into morning and vice versa, so you must decide to break that cycle that you are drowning in, and it was not easy at first to reset your Circadian, but with some steps, you may finally succeed in overcoming Depression without medication. Set a specific time to wake up and sleep, do not change it no matter what happens, and set the alarm on it.

Avoid any distractions, be it electronic devices or television.

Make sure the room is quiet, lightly lit, and free of any sound. Try reading a book before bed to get you to relax quickly.

Music- treatment: Music has a tremendous ability to penetrate and reach the depths of the human soul.

So don't be surprised if you see that some people shed tears when they listen to a piece of music. Music has a tremendous ability to bring out different moods and depressions, and the reason for this is that music is closely related to a personal experience or personal event.

Therefore, we find that the listener associates the musical piece he hears with the perception or subjective feelings. Therefore, we always find that when we want to go through the same moment and feelings, we resort to listening to a specific song or piece of music.

Types of depression treatment with music:

Where the psychiatrist asks the person to produce a group of music clips or songs related to his life, and this group is divided into 3 types:

First type:

It is a group of music clips or songs that make you feel sad, or in a more correct sense, that affect their depression, often these songs are songs or music with a slow rhythm, or what is called dark music, these songs must have an impression on the person to the past.

The second type:

It is a collection of songs and musical pieces that make a person mood swings, or suitable for transformation. Often this music is not happy or sad, but rather appropriate to the situation in which the person lives, but do not forget that such songs must mean something to me. the person.

The third type:

It is a collection of songs and musical pieces that bring a person back to moments of happiness.

Often these pieces of music have a fast tempo, and their music is full of feelings and vitality and sends more joy and joy to the person who hears them, and after the person compiles these songs and musical pieces on his own disc, he is asked

to hear these songs in the same previous order And this process is repeated several times a week, for a few weeks, and over time the person will discover that there is a clear improvement in his condition, and he was able to get rid of the depression that dominates his condition.

He will feel a group of abundant feelings for as long as possible, and perhaps dear reader, you will discover that such a method takes a long time, perhaps up to a whole day until a person can collect these songs, but what is the problem if these songs or music will contribute to improving His condition is depressed.

Pet therapy:

Before entering into the details of the quality of this type of treatment, we should make it clear that pets send an atmosphere of reassurance and comfort to their owners.

_ I know you are asking, dear reader, how do pets affect depression treatment?

_Owning a pet reduces stress and tension.

_Owning a pet increases the general sense of health and well-being of the owner of this animal.

_Visibly improves the patient's mood.

_It was found that for people with heart attacks, the rate of recurrence of the _attack during the first-year decreases by five times if these people own pets.

Pets have feelings and needs, and therefore you will feel that there is a living being who shares your needs and your daily life.

Writing: helps in analysing difficult experiences, thoughts, and feelings, and thus leads to an increase in the individual's self-understanding. Some patients recovering from depression report that, by simply writing and reading their own thoughts they set out to understand the causes behind their illness.

Sunlight treatment: Many people suffer from seasonal depression that is associated with the seasons of the year, especially in the fall and winter seasons. The main reason for this depression is the lack of natural light.

It has become clear to psychiatrists that the severe decrease in the brightness of the light in the autumn and winter seasons is a major factor in causing psychological depression in many people. Because when the light flows well through the retina, the information is sent to the brain, so the brain directly tells the body to produce more serotonin.

Serotonin's primary function is to regulate the neurotransmitters involved in sleep, appetite, and memory. Thus, this regulation is reflected in the mood to turn into a good one.

That is why psychotherapists often recommend that we expose ourselves to sunlight every day for between 30 and 60 minutes.

Even if our general mood is not receptive to this idea because of the depression that dominates us, it is necessary to make an effort to help ourselves overcome severe depression (black acute depression).

Make the room a place to treat depression: It is natural and obvious that our room when we suffer from depression is like a dark cave, and this is what all those who succumb to depression do. They tend to be isolated and withdrawn inside the room, not to mention shutting windows and not being able to stand the lights. This is very understandable and justified, because the depressed does not feel any taste of life, and becomes indifferent to many things that some may despise.

But as we agreed, we must help ourselves to get rid of depression, certainly, it is not that easy, but what I know and everyone knows is that it is not impossible, if you find the will to recover from depression, you will certainly overcome it, and will even turn into an assistant to others who are struggling to get out from the maze of depression.

A little effort and will to make our living room a natural medicine for depression, let the windows open, and get rid of that darkness that makes depression dig deep inside you. Get up and tidy up the room and put everything in its place.

Let them smell good, put perfume on the window blinds, on the covers, and a little on the pillow. Try to get a small electric incense burner if you don't have it, and leave it running all the time to make the room air fresher.

Switch the places of everything in your room. For example, make your bed near the window to inhale the oxygen when you leave it open some times during the day. Change the place of the table, and try not to do your work while you are in bed.

Bed and lying on it all day are taboo for a depressed person because it makes depression dig deep inside you. Try to sit behind the table in

order to do your homework or do your business. And do not forget to try to get a white rose that you put in a small cup in front of you. Even if there is no one around you to buy it for you, go and buy it yourself, its effect is exactly the same as that of an antidepressant pill.

The end

In the end, I would like to say that you are the most capable of all who can help to get rid of depression, a little effort and will, will give you results that you did not expect in defeating depression.

remember:

Many depression patients have recovered because of their will and passion, so I want you to be one of them. You are not alone. This book is made for you to help you.

…………...

Notes:

Notes:

Notes:

Notes:

Notes: